DICTIONARY

A complete reference guide containing
the Percussive Arts Society's
40 International Drum Rudiments

JAY WANAMAKER

INCLUDES:
Practice Patterns
Rudimental Snare Drum Solos

Cover photograph by Karen Miller

Copyright © MMII by Alfred Music Publishing Co., Inc.
All Rights Reserved. Printed in USA.
ISBN-10: 0-7390-2732-8
ISBN-13: 978-0-7390-2732-5

CONTENTS

SEVEN ESSENTIAL RUDIMENTS

Knowledge of the Seven Essential Rudiments is necessary in order to perform all the other rudiments. They are listed below, in suggested teaching order. All rudiments should be practiced in the following manner: open (slow), to closed (fast), to open (slow), and/or at an even, moderate march tempo.

SINGLE STROKE ROLL

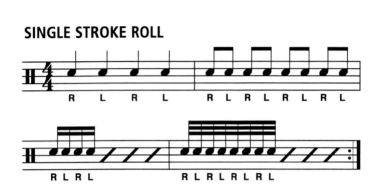

MULTIPLE BOUNCE ROLL

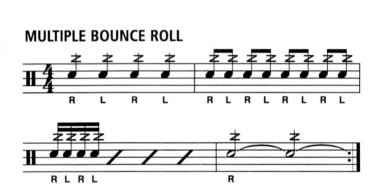

DOUBLE STROKE OPEN ROLL

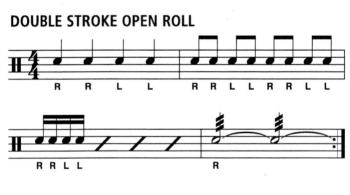

FIVE STROKE ROLL

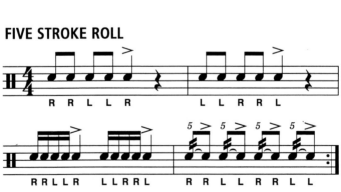

SINGLE PARADIDDLE

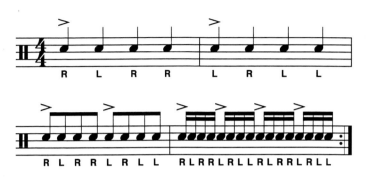

FLAM

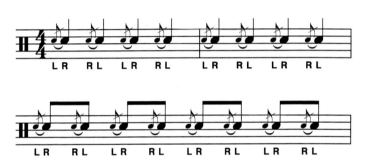

DRAG

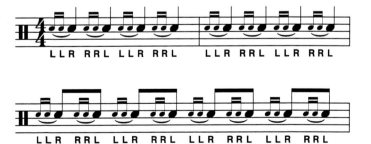

ROLL RUDIMENTS

Single Stroke Roll Rudiments

1. SINGLE STROKE ROLL

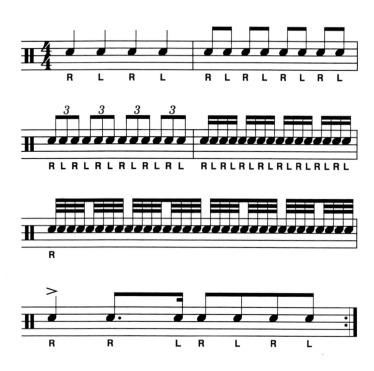

2. SINGLE STROKE FOUR (Four Stroke Ruff)

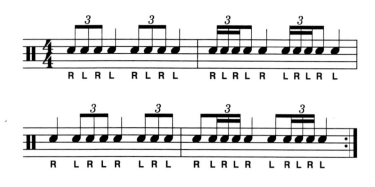

3. SINGLE STROKE SEVEN

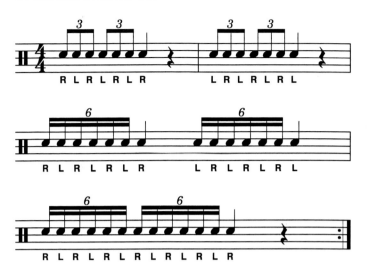

Multiple Bounce Roll Rudiments

4. MULTIPLE BOUNCE ROLL
(Buzz, Orchestral, and Press Rolls)

Duple Pulsation

Interpreted:

Triple Pulsation

5. TRIPLE STROKE ROLL

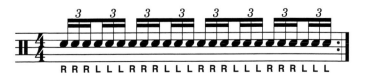

Double Stroke Open Roll Rudiments

6. DOUBLE STROKE OPEN ROLL (Long Roll)

Duple Pulsation

Interpreted:

RR LL RR LL RR LL RR LL RR LL RR LL RR LL RR LL RR LL

Practice Procedure

R R R R R   R R R R   L L L L L   L L L L
L L L L L   L L L L   R R R R R   R R R R

R R R R R   R R R R R   R R R   R R R R R R
L L L L L   L L L L L   L L L   L L L L L L

Triple Pulsation

Interpreted:

RR LL RR LL RR LL RR LL RR LL RR LL

Practice Procedure

R R L L R R L L   R R L L R R L L R R L L

R R L L R R L L R R L L R R L L

RRLLRRLLRRLLRRLL RRLLRRLLRRLLRRLLRRLLRRLLR

7. FIVE STROKE ROLL

R L R L R L R L R L R L   RRLLR LLRRL RRLLR LLRRL

R L R L R L R L R L R L   R LLRRL RRLLR LLRRL

8. SIX STROKE ROLL

R L R L R   L R L R L

R LLRR L R   L RRLL R L

RRLL R L   RRLL R L   RRLL R L   RRLL R L

Variation No. 2

R L RRLL R L RRLL R L RRLL R L RRLL

9. SEVEN STROKE ROLL

R L R L R L R L R L R L R L R L R L

Duple Pulsation

RRLLRR L RRLLRR L RRLLRR L RRLLRRL

Tap Seven Stroke Roll

R LLRRLL R LLRRLL R LLRRLL R LLRRLL

Triple Pulsation

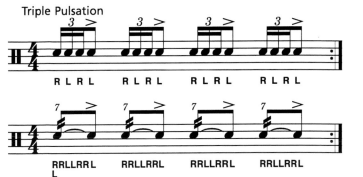

R L R L   R L R L   R L R L   R L R L

RRLLRRL   RRLLRRL   RRLLRRL   RRLLRRL
L

10. NINE STROKE ROLL

R L R L R   L R L R L   RRLLRRLLR LLRRLLRRL

11. TEN STROKE ROLL

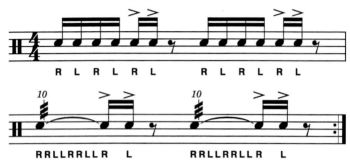

R L R L R L   R L R L R L

RRLLRRLLR   L   RRLLRRLLR   L

12. ELEVEN STROKE ROLL

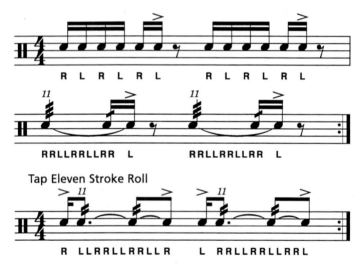

R L R L R L   R L R L R L

RRLLRRLLRR   L   RRLLRRLLRR   L

Tap Eleven Stroke Roll

R   LLRRLLRRLLR   L   RRLLRRLLRRL

13. THIRTEEN STROKE ROLL

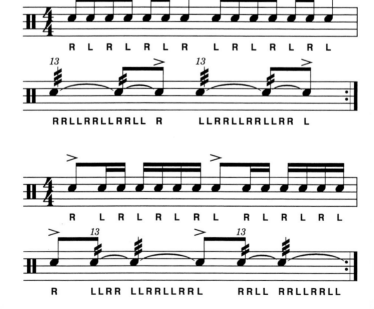

R L R L R L R   L R L R L R L

RRLLRRLLRRLL R   LLRRLLRRLLRR L

R   L R L R L R L   R L R L R L

R   LLRR LLRRLLRRL   RRLL RRLLRRLL

14. FIFTEEN STROKE ROLL

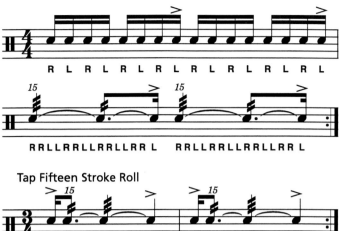

R L R L R L R L R L R L R L R L

R R L L R R L L R R L L R R L   R R L L R R L L R R L L R R L

Tap Fifteen Stroke Roll

R L L R R L L R R L L R R L R   L R R L L R R L L R R L L R R L

15. SEVENTEEN STROKE ROLL

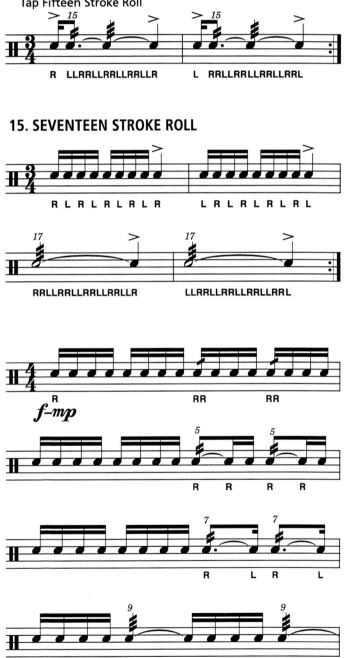

R L R L R L R L R   L R L R L R L R L

R R L L R R L L R R L L R R L L R   L L R R L L R R L L R R L L R R L

R   RR   RR

f–*mp*

R   R   R   R

R   L R   L

R   R   R

R   R   R R RR R R

Rollin'
(Summary Solo)

Jay Wanamaker

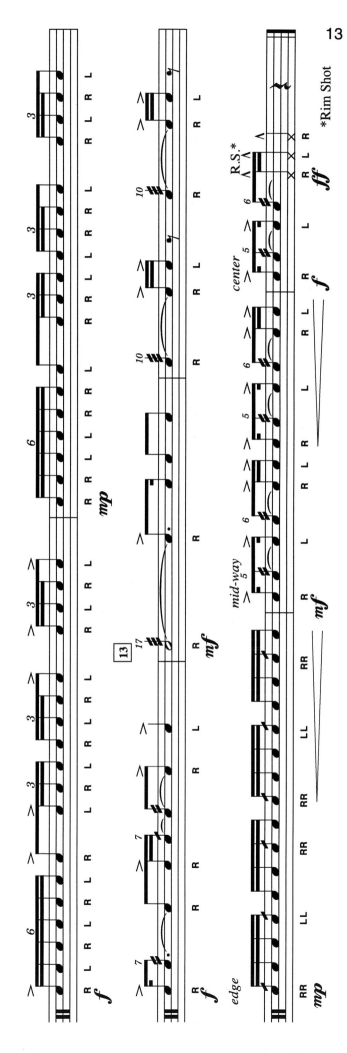

13

*Rim Shot

Diddle Rudiments

16. SINGLE PARADIDDLE

R L R R L R L L

R L R R L R L L R L R R L R L L

Paradiddle Inversions
♩ = 126

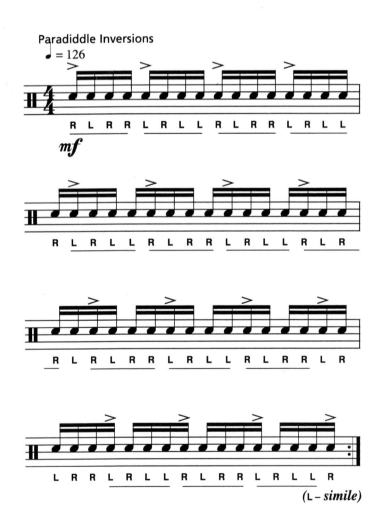

R L R R L R L L R L R R L R L L

mf

R L R L L L R L R R L R L L L R L R

R L R L R R L R L L R L R R L R

L R R L R L L L R L R R L R L L R

(L – *simile*)

Paradiddle Shifting Accent and Inversion Study

♩ = 126

R L R R L R L L R L R R L R L L

mf

R L R R L R L L R L R R L R L L

R L R L L R L R R L R L L R L R

R R L R L L R L R R L R L L R L

R R L R L L R L R R L R L L R L

R L L R L R R L R L L R L R R L

R L R R L R L L R L R R L R L L

17. DOUBLE PARADIDDLE

R L R L R R   L R L R L L

RLRLRRLRLRLL   RLRLRRLRLRLL

18. TRIPLE PARADIDDLE

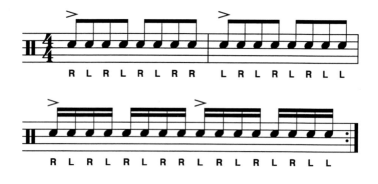

R L R L R L R R   L R L R L R L L

R L R L R L R R L R L R L R L R L L

19. SINGLE PARADIDDLE-DIDDLE

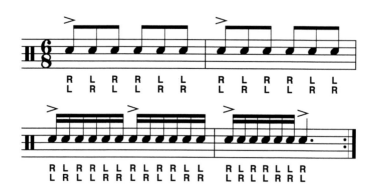

R L R R L L   R L R R L L
L R L L R R   L R L L R R

RLRRLLRLRRLL   RLRRLLR
LRLLRRLRLLRR   LRLLRRL

Paradiddle Accent Study

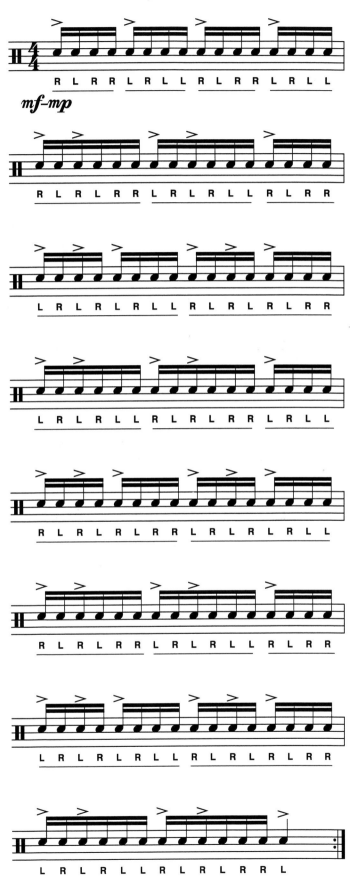

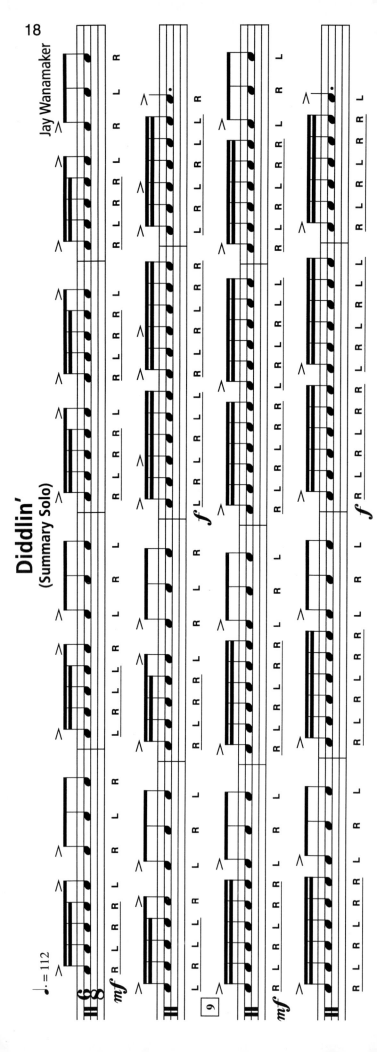

Diddlin'
(Summary Solo)

Jay Wanamaker

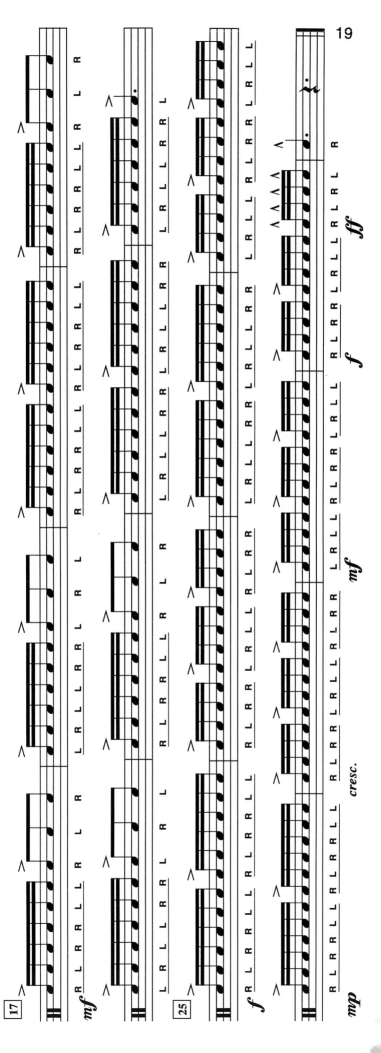

Flam Rudiments

20. FLAM

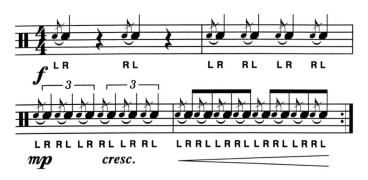

21. FLAM ACCENT

22. FLAM TAP

Variation

Practice Procedure

23. FLAMACUE

LR L R LLR   LR L R LLR

LR L R LLR   LR L R LLR

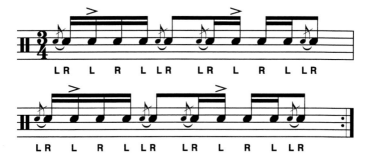

LR L R L LR   LR L R L LR

LR L R LLR   LR L R L LR

24. FLAM PARADIDDLE

LR L R R RL R L L

LR L R RRL R L LLR L R RRL R L L

Practice Procedure

R   R R R   R   R R L
L   L L L   L   L L L

25. SINGLE FLAMMED MILL

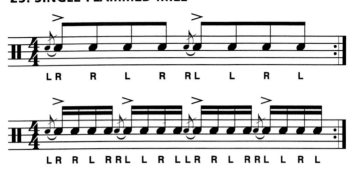

LR   R   L   R   RL   L   R   L

LR R L RRL L R LLR R L RRL L R L

Practice Procedure

RR RR R RR RR R   L L LL LL L LL L

Single Flammed Mill Summary

LR R L RRL L R LLR R L RRL L R L

R LLR R L RRL L R LLR R L RRL

26. FLAM PARADIDDLE-DIDDLE

LR L R R L L   RL R L L R R

LR L R R L L RL R L L R R

LR L R R L L RL R L L R R

Practice Procedure

R R R   RR   RR R R   RR   RR

LL   LLL LL   LL   LLL LL

27. PATAFLAFLA

Variation

Pataflafla Summary

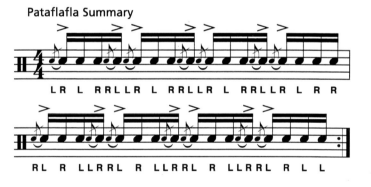

Practice Procedure

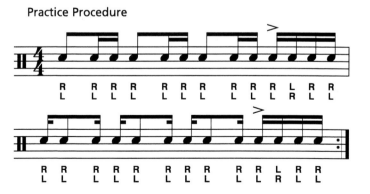

28. SWISS ARMY TRIPLET

Practice Procedure

Swiss Army Triplet Summary

29. INVERTED FLAM TAP

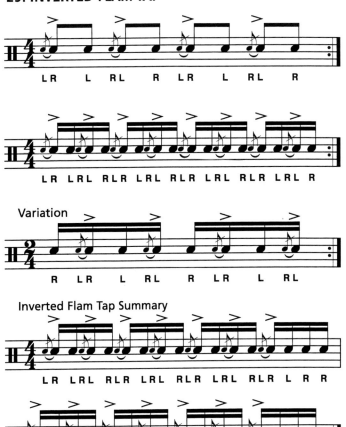

Variation

Inverted Flam Tap Summary

30. FLAM DRAG

Flam It
(Summary Solo)

Jay Wanamaker

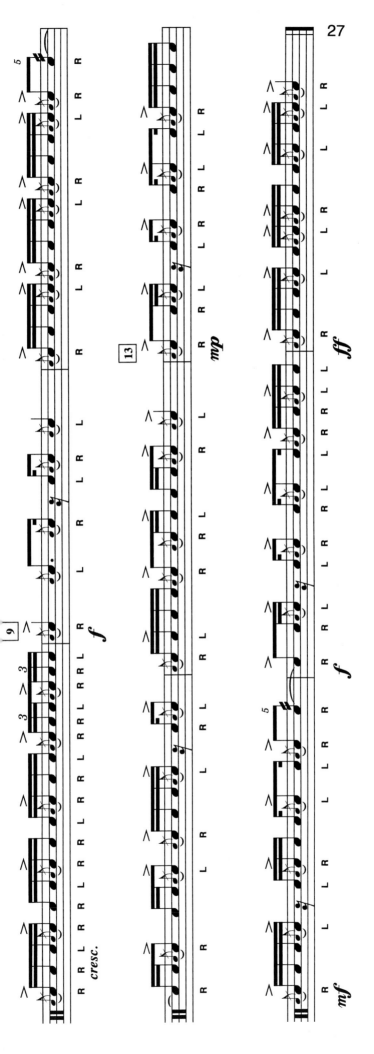

Drag Rudiments

Depending on the interpretation, all grace notes in the following examples can be played in either an open or closed manner.

31. DRAG

L L R   R R L   L L R   R R L

Non-Alternating Drags

L L R   L L R   L L R   L L R

R R L   R R L   R R L   R R L

32. SINGLE DRAG TAP

L L R   L   R R L   R

L L R   L R R L   R L L R   L R R L   R

R   L L R   L   R R L   R   L L R   L   R R L

R   L L R   L   R R L   R   L L R   L   R R L

Variation

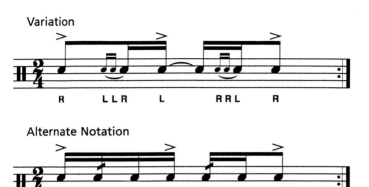

R   L L R   L   R R L   R

Alternate Notation

R   LL   R   L   RR   L   R

33. DOUBLE DRAG TAP

L L R L L R   L   R R L R R L   R

L L R   L L R   L   R R L   R R L   R

Variation No. 1

L L R   L L R   L R R L   R R L   R

Variation No. 2

R   L L R   L L R   L   R R L   R R L   R

Alternate Notation

R   LL   R   LL   R   L   RR   L   RR   L   R

34. LESSON 25

LLR L R LLR L R
RRL R L RRL R L

Variation

R LLR L R LLR L
L RRL R L RRL R

Alternate Notation

R LL R L R LL R L

35. SINGLE DRAGADIDDLE

RR L R R LL R L L RR L R R LL R L L

Single Dragadiddle Summary

RR L R R LL R L L RR L R R LL R L L

R L RR L R R LL R L L RR L R R L

36. DRAG PARADIDDLE NO. 1

R LLR L R R   L RRL R L L

R LLR L R R L RRL R L L

Alternate Notation

R LL R L R R L RR L R L L

37. DRAG PARADIDDLE NO. 2

R LLRLLR L R R   L RRL RRL R L L

R LLRLLR L R R L RRL RRL R L L

Alternate Notation

R LL R LL R L R R L RR L RR L R L L

38. SINGLE RATAMACUE

LLR L R L RRL R L R

LLR L R L RRL R L R

Variation

R LLR L R L RRL R L

Alternate Notation

R LL R L R L RR L R L

39. DOUBLE RATAMACUE

LLR LLR L R L RRL RRL R L R

LLR LLR L R L RRL RRL R L R

Variation

R LLR LLR L R L RRL RRL R L

Alternate Notation

R LL R LL R L R L RR L RR L R L

40. TRIPLE RATAMACUE

LLR LLR LLR L R L   RRL RRL RRL R L R

LLR LLR LLR L R L RRL RRL RRL R L R

Variation

R LLR LLR LLR L R L RRL RRL RRL R L

Alternate Notation

R LL R LL R LL R L R L RR L RR L RR L R L

Ratamacue Summary

R LLR L R L   R LLR L R L

R LLR L R L RRL RRL R L R   L

LLR LLR L R L RRL RRL R L R LLR L R L

RRL RRL RRL R L R LLR L R L   R

It's a Drag
(Summary Solo)

Jay Wanamaker

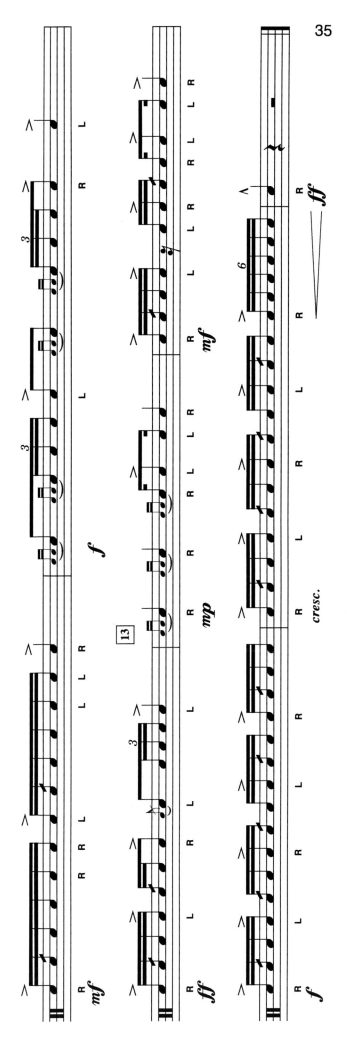

Chops
(Final Rudimental Solo)

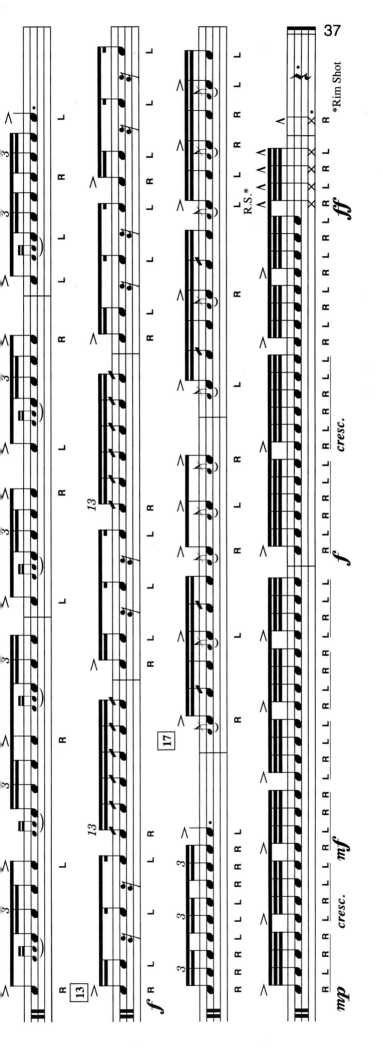

PERCUSSIVE ARTS SOCIETY INTERNATIONAL DRUM RUDIMENTS

All rudiments should be practiced as follows: open (slow), to closed (fast), to open (slow), and/or at an even, moderate march tempo.

Roll Rudiments

SINGLE STROKE ROLL RUDIMENTS

1. Single Stroke Roll*

2. Single Stroke Four

3. Single Stroke Seven

MULTIPLE BOUNCE ROLL RUDIMENTS

4. Multiple Bounce Roll

5. Triple Stroke Roll

DOUBLE STROKE OPEN ROLL RUDIMENTS

6. Double Stroke Open Roll*

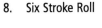

7. Five Stroke Roll*

8. Six Stroke Roll

9. Seven Stroke Roll*

10. Nine Stroke Roll*

11. Ten Stroke Roll*

12. Eleven Stroke Roll*

13. Thirteen Stroke Roll*

14. Fifteen Stroke Roll*

R
L

L R
R L

L
R

15. Seventeen Stroke Roll

R

R

L

L

Diddle Rudiments

16. Single Paradiddle*

R L R R L R L L

17. Double Paradiddle*

R L R L R R L R L R L L

18. Triple Paradiddle

R L R L R L R R L R L R L R L L

19. Single Paradiddle-Diddle

R L R R L L R L R R L L
L R L L R R L R L L R R

Flam Rudiments

20. Flam*

L R   R L

21. Flam Accent*

L R   L   R   R L   R   L

22. Flam Tap*

L R   R R L   L L R   R R L   L

23. Flamacue*

L R   L   R   L   L R
R L   R   L   R   R L

24. Flam Paradiddle*

L R   L   R   R R L   R   L   L

25. Single Flammed Mill

L R   R   L   R R L   L   R   L

26. Flam Paradiddle-Diddle*

L R L R R L L R L R L L R R

27. Pataflafla

L R   L   R R L L R   L   R R L

28. Swiss Army Triplet

L R   R   L L R   R   L
R L   L   R R L   L   R

29. Inverted Flam Tap

L R   L R L   R L R   L R L   R

30. Flam Drag

L R   L   L R R L   R R L

---

* These rudiments are also included in the original
   Standard 26 American Drum Rudiments.

Drag Rudiments

31. Drag*

LLR   RRL

32. Single Drag Tap*

LLR   L RRL   R

33. Double Drag Tap*

LLRLLR   LRRLRRL   R

34. Lesson 25*

LLR L R LLR L R
RRL R L RRL R L

35. Single Dragadiddle

RR L R R LL R L L

36. Drag Paradiddle No. 1*

R LLR L R R L RRL R L L

37. Drag Paradiddle No. 2*

R LLR LLR L R R L RRL RRL R L L

38. Single Ratamacue*

LLR L R L RRL R L R

39. Double Ratamacue*

LLR LLR L R L RRL RRL R L R

40. Triple Ratamacue*

LLR LLR LLR L R L RRL RRL RRL R L R

A recording of the International Drum Rudiments as performed by Rob Carson, the three-time World Snare Drum Champion, is available from Alfred Music Publishing Co., Inc. (item 18049).